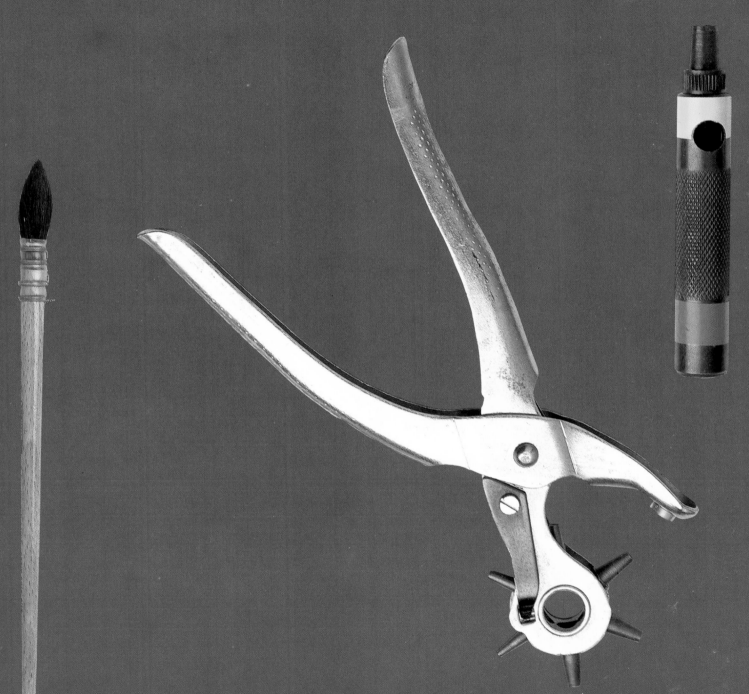

# A Gallery of Games

by Catherine Marchon-Arnaud
photographs by Marc Schwartz
research by Etienne Collomb

series under the direction
of Caroline Lancrenon

TICKNOR & FIELDS
New York • 1994

# CONTENTS

# A NOTE TO THE READER

This is a book of games to make and play. Many of them are familiar, because they are thousands of years old and have been played (with variations) all over the world. People have been playing games like these since before the beginning of recorded history!

There are just a few things to keep in mind when using this book:

• Some of the projects require the use of an X-acto knife. These are extremely sharp (much sharper than most kitchen knives) and should be used carefully. Anyone who is using an X-acto knife for the first time should ask an adult for help.

• When cutting anything with a knife, always put a wooden board or thick cardboard underneath. That protects the work surface, and also provides a smooth cutting surface.

• Whenever a project requires paint, glue, or clay, cover the work surface with newspaper before starting.

• When using a strong glue (such as Super Glue), squeeze it directly from the tube. Wipe off any excess glue with a cloth. A drop or two is usually enough.

• It isn't necessary to make the games look exactly like the ones in the pictures. Use this as a book of ideas and suggestions, and be willing to experiment!

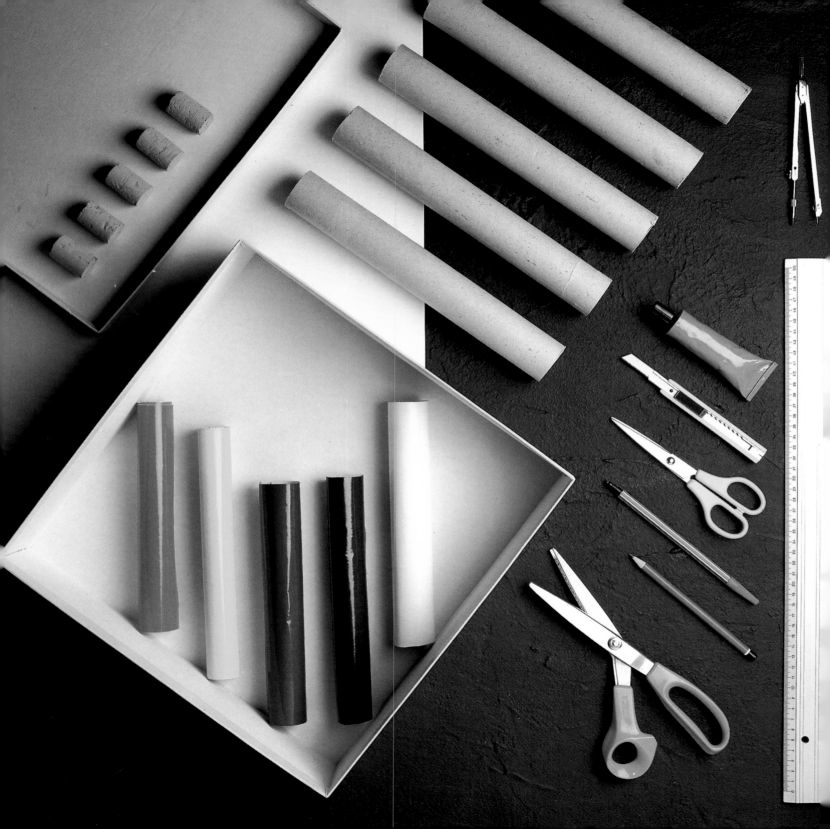

# GIFT BOX RING TOSS

## Equipment

- 1 square gift box
- 5 cardboard tubes (from paper towels or aluminum foil)
- 1 sheet of white tagboard (20 x 26 inches)
- 5 large pieces of contact paper (different colors)
- 5 wide corks
- 2B pencil (soft lead)
- glue
- X-acto knife
- scissors
- pinking shears
- drawing compass
- ruler

a hole in the top of the shoe box. Push it through until it touches the bottom of the box and twist it back and forth so that the pencil traces a circle on the bottom of the box. Repeat this process for each hole.

**2**

Remove the cover and glue a cork in the center of each circle on the bottom of the box. (These are to stabilize the tubes.) Put the cover back on.

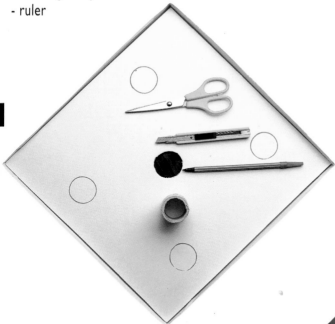

**3**

Place a cardboard tube on the inside of the box cover and trace around it 5 times, as shown. Carefully cut out the holes with the knife. Put the top back on the box. With the pencil, darken the end of the cardboard tube. Slide the tube through

Decorate the tubes and the box with strips of contact paper.

**4**

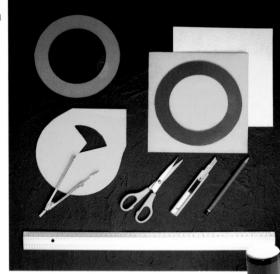

To make the rings, cut nine 8-inch squares out of the tagboard. Put contact paper on both sides of each. Draw 2 diagonal lines (from corner to corner) across one of the squares. Placing the pointed end of the compass on the spot where the lines cross, draw a circle that is 7 inches in diameter (a 3 1/2-inch radius). Then draw another circle inside this one, 5 inches in diameter (a 2 1/2-inch radius). Use the knife to cut a small triangle out of the center; this will make it easier to cut out the inside of the circle with scissors. After cutting out 1 ring, use this circle as a pattern to mark and cut out the other rings (3 of each color—9 in all).

**Store the tubes and the rings inside the box after the game.**

Place each tube in a hole in the cover. Make each tube worth a different number of points.

## RULES OF THE GAME

Each player uses a set of rings of a particular color. One at a time, the players stand a set distance from the box and throw the rings around the tubes. The player with the most points wins.

# WOODEN PEG RING TOSS

## Equipment

- 2–3 wood dowels or broom handles cut into 5 pieces (each at least 24 inches long)
- 22 feet of lightweight plastic hose with a small diameter
- 3–4 bamboo pieces or 12 thin corks (to fit tightly inside the hose)
- flat brush
- cloth tape (5 different colors)
- strong glue
- poster paint in 6 different colors (optional)
- ruler
- X-acto knife with straight blade
- X-acto knife with serrated blade (or small saw)
- scissors

**Insert pegs into the ground outside, and play according to the rules on page 10. Each peg should be worth a different number of points.**

To make rings, cut twelve 22-inch pieces of hose. Using the knife with a serrated blade, cut twelve 1-inch pieces of bamboo or use corks. Glue half the bamboo piece or cork inside the hose, then glue the other end of the hose to the protruding end of bamboo or cork. Hold it together until the glue dries. Cover the joint with cloth tape. Each player should have 2 rings, so use different colors of tape to distinguish the sets.

Paint dowels in different colors or wrap with colored tape to make pegs.

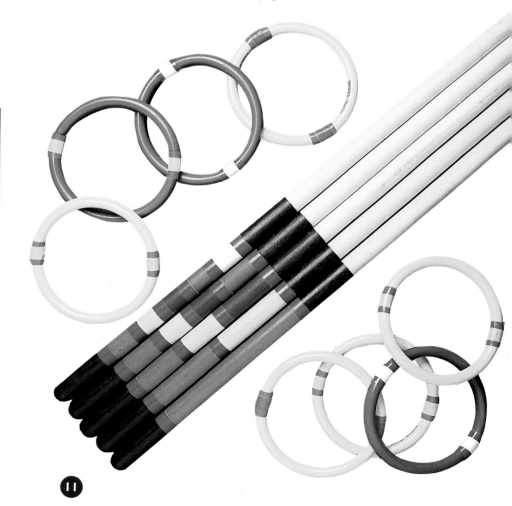

# TIN CAN TOSS

**Equipment**
- 8 empty cans of the same diameter but different heights, lids and labels removed
- 5 pieces of contact paper (different colors)
- several sheets of graph paper
- Ping-Pong balls
- pencil
- felt-tip pen
- strong glue
- scissors
- ruler

# BRANCH-AND-STICK RING TOSS

**Equipment**
- 8–10 thin, flexible branches or vines (willow, ivy) about 1/2 inch in diameter and 12 inches long
- 6–8 thick branches or pieces of bamboo
- pebbles

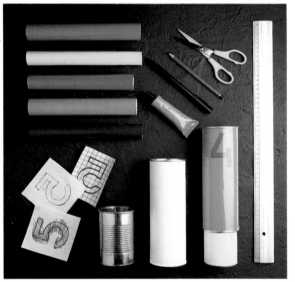

**Use Ping-Pong balls or other light plastic balls to play this game.**

Glue 3 tall cans and 3 short cans together to make different heights. Cover each can with contact paper, including the one tall can and one short can that have not been glued to each other. Draw a number on the graph paper with a felt-tip pen and transfer it to the backing of the contact paper. Cut out the number and attach it to the can. Position the cans as shown and glue them all together.

Remove the leaves from the branches and twist stems together to make rings.
Cut 24-inch pegs from the bamboo or thick branches. Push them into dirt or sand. Place pebbles at the base of each branch to indicate how many points it is worth.

Games of skill are played everywhere in the world. Some of them are as old as the earliest recorded history.

Knucklebones (jacks or dice made from bones), clay marbles, and balls made from pigs' bladders were common among the ancient Egyptians, Greeks, and Romans.

## BOWLING AND SKITTLES

Bowling is one of the oldest games of skill. Historically, it was often played with nine pins, not ten. The earlier game was called skittles or ninepins and sometimes played by throwing a disk, not a ball, at the pins. The tenth pin was added in the nineteenth century. Connecticut had passed a law prohibiting ninepins because too many people were betting on the game. Adding a tenth pin made the game legal!

## THE OLDEST BOWLING GAME IN THE WORLD

In 1895 the archaeologist Sir Flinders Petric discovered the tomb of a young child in Nagada, Egypt. Inside this tomb, built in 5200 B.C., was the oldest complete bowling game ever found. It consisted of nine small stone vases, three marble blocks, and four stone balls. When the game was played, the three blocks were set up to form an arch. The players rolled the ball through the arch to knock down the vases.

## BOWLING GAMES AROUND THE WORLD

Bowling, skittles, and similar games are played all over the world and by many different sets of rules. In the United States, bowling consists of rolling a large ball down a sixty-foot-long alley to knock down ten pins. *Bowls*, in England, is played on a lawn. Players throw a wooden ball sixty to ninety feet and try to hit a target ball (called a jack). Another related game, which the French call *boules* and Italian call *bocci*, is thousands of years old. This game also requires the players to throw a ball at a smaller target ball. In Germany, over one thousand years ago, people played a bowling game in church. Players rolled a ball down the long church cloister and tried to knock down a wooden club. If they could knock down the club, they were cleansed of their sins.

Greek art. Terra-cotta sculpture. *Girls Playing Knucklebones.*

## ANCIENT GAMES

The Greeks often played *cottabus* at the end of their banquets. The game consisted of throwing the last few drops of wine in a glass at a target chosen by the guests—generally a vase or a plate. If any wine was spilled the player was disqualified, but the wine was supposed to make a loud splashing noise when it hit the target.

*Ascolia* was a Roman game that required a great deal of agility. One by one the guests had to balance themselves on a goatskin wine bottle for as long as they could. The winner received the contents of the bottle.

## DANGEROUS GAMES

During the fifteenth and sixteenth centuries, games of skill were often based on balancing exercises. Favorite games included sitting on a stick balanced above a large tub or hopping with a halberd (a combination spear and battle-ax) balanced on the participant's nose. Aside from these dangerous games, skittles was also fashionable.

Portrait believed to be Louis XVII playing with an *émigrette* (yo-yo).

## THE YO-YO

This toy has a long history. It was depicted on the ceramics of ancient Greece and was both a toy and a weapon in the Philippines. The word *yo-yo* comes from the Philippine word meaning "to return." The yo-yo was particularly popular among the French aristocracy who escaped the French Revolution. At the time the French called the toy the *émigrette* (refugee).

# FLOWERPOT SOLITAIRE

### Equipment

- 1 clay flowerpot tray (about 9 inches in diameter)
- 1 plate or salad bowl (same diameter as tray)
- 1 sheet of white tagboard (1/8 inch thick)
- 1 sheet of graph paper
- 4 sheets of strong construction paper (different colors)
- 1 piece of synthetic raffia or green felt
- 33 rubber washers, 1 inch in diameter (available in hardware stores) or 33 brown paper circles of same size
- 33 thumbtacks (yellow, white, pink, red)
- wooden toothpicks
- coin (quarter)
- brown acrylic paint
- brush
- pencil
- roll of green floral tape
- pinking shears
- strong glue
- scissors
- crewel embroidery needle

Raffia and floral tape are sold in garden-supply stores.

# RULES OF THE GAME

Remove the piece in the middle of the board. The goal is to remove all but one of the pieces by jumping over them. Captures are made by jumping over an adjacent piece and removing it. Any piece may jump over any piece next to it, but pieces may be moved only when jumping. Continue playing until all possible captures have been made. To make the game even harder, try to finish with the last remaining piece in the middle of the board.

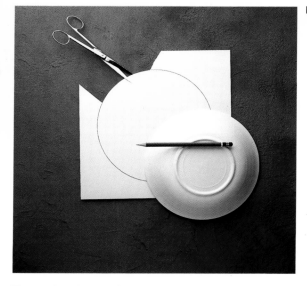

**1**

Trace the shape of the plate or bowl on the tagboard and cut it out.

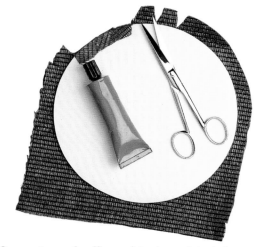

**2**

Cut a piece of raffia or felt about 1 inch larger than the circle. Coat the tagboard with glue and attach the raffia to it. Cut notches around the edge of the raffia. Place a line of glue on the back of the tagboard circle and glue down the notched edges of the raffia.

**3**

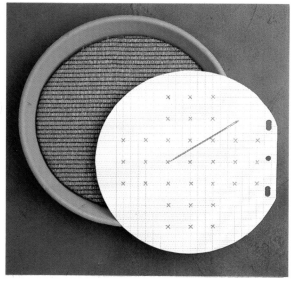

Spread glue all around the edge of the raffia-covered circle and carefully place it in the clay tray (hold in place until it dries). Trace around the plate on the graph paper and cut out the circle. Mark Xs as shown. Place the graph paper on the raffia and mark each point with the embroidery needle, pressing through the tagboard.

**4**

Glue the rubber washers around each of the holes in the raffia, making sure each hole is in the middle of a washer.

**5**

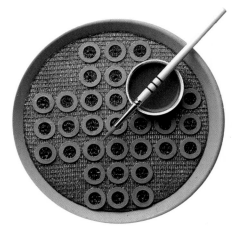

Paint the center of each washer brown.

**6**

Cut thirty-two 2-inch squares from the colored paper and trace a circle on each one using the quarter. Then use the pinking shears to cut out the circles. Place a thumbtack through center of a circle. Hold the point while you cut each notch to head of tack with the regular scissors (see photograph). Repeat for all the other circles. Leave tacks sticking through paper flowers.

If floral tape is unavailable, color the toothpick green with paint or felt-tip pen, and attach thumbtack to it by wrapping the end with clear tape.

With the scissors, cut off one point from each toothpick. Attach the thumbtack (with the flower) to the cut end of the toothpick. Wrap floral tape around the toothpick and tack. Repeat for each.

# SOLITAIRE ON A NOTEBOOK DIVIDER

### Equipment
- 1 stiff plastic or cardboard divider for large notebook
- 1 sheet of graph paper
- 33 marbles
- pencil
- hole punch
- hammer

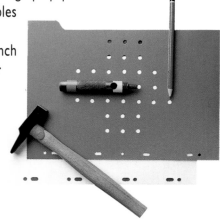

Make a grid in the shape of a cross on the graph paper. Place the graph paper on the divider and press hard on each point with a pencil to mark the position of the holes. Use the punch and hammer to make the holes.

# JEANS POCKET SOLITAIRE

## Equipment

- 1 jeans patch pocket (or piece of denim or other heavy fabric cut in the shape of a pocket)
- 1 sheet of graph paper
- heat-bonding fabric or needle and thread
- 1 wooden barbecue skewer
- 1 blue felt-tip pen
- eyelet kit
- crewel embroidery needle
- chalk
- X-acto knife

Trace a grid in the shape of a cross on the graph paper. Place this grid on the pocket and push the needle through the paper and jeans pocket to mark the points. Then rub each point with chalk through the pattern. Place an eyelet on each point and attach with pliers of eyelet kit. Attach the pocket to jeans with heat-bonding fabric, sew it by hand, or ask an adult to sew it by machine.
With the knife, cut 3/4-inch-long pieces of the skewer. Use the felt-tip pen to paint half of each one blue.

Before playing, put 2 pens in the pocket, 1 along each side—otherwise, the pegs won't stand up straight. Keep the pegs in the pocket when not playing.

# PIE DOUGH SOLITAIRE

To make an unusual solitaire game, mix 4 cups of flour, 2 cups of salt, and 2 cups of warm water. Place the dough in a lightly oiled pie pan. Place 33 marbles in a cross shape in the dough, pushing them in slightly (see photograph). Cook at 350°F for 30 minutes. Cool until marbles can be touched, then remove the marbles and put the dough back in the oven for 30 minutes more. Reduce the heat to 200°F and bake for another hour. Use marbles, candy, or fruit as game pieces.

Solitaire games—games played by a single player—have different names in different parts of the world. The British call solitaire played with cards *patience*. When the British and French say "solitaire," they mean solitaire played on a board with pegs or marbles.

Tiddlywinks.
France, about 1900.

## Origins

Solitaire games have been played for so many years, in so many places, that no one knows when and where they began. Two thousand years ago, the Latin poet Ovid mentioned a game similar to solitaire.

Peg solitaire probably appeared in the seventeenth century. Legend says that a version of the game was invented by a man imprisoned in the terrible Bastille in Paris, who was looking for a way to pass the time in his prison cell.

A variation on the game of Chinese checkers, which is a combination solitaire and checkers game, was probably played in ancient China.

Game of War.
Germany, about 1860.

## JIGSAW PUZZLES

Jigsaw puzzles are named for a tool once used to cut them out—the jigsaw—which is ideal for cutting fine lines and sharp curves in wood.

In the late eighteenth century, a Frenchman and an Englishman each had the idea of selling cut-up maps that had to be reassembled. They were a success, and other merchants were soon selling cut-up pictures of historical scenes, animals, plants, and alphabets. All of these early puzzles were sold as educational devices.

In the nineteenth century, puzzles were mass produced for the first time, making them less expensive. This was also the first time manufacturers were able to print puzzles in color. (Earlier puzzles had to be printed in black and white and then colored by hand.) Some of the nineteenth-century puzzles showed pictures from nursery rhymes and fairy tales—they were meant to be fun, not educational.

Jigsaw puzzle called *The Hunt.* France, about 1850.

Modern puzzles can have as many as ten thousand pieces and all kinds of pictures. There are even some puzzles whose pieces are all the same color! Recent developments in jigsaw puzzles include double-sided puzzles, which have a different picture on each side, and—newest of all—three-dimensional jigsaws that form a model of a building.

Chinese tangram puzzles can be played alone or against an opponent. The goal is to take the seven pieces (triangles and four-sided figures cut from a single square) and put them together to form different shapes.

## CARDS

Playing cards probably originated in the Middle East or China, arrived in Venice, and then spread to Germany and France. The oldest known deck of cards dates from 1430.

Three main types of cards soon developed: Italian (with suits of swords, cups, rings, and batons), German (bells, hearts, leaves, and acorns), and French (hearts, spades, clubs, and diamonds). The last, of course, is the type used for most card games in the United States.

## SOLITAIRE AND PATIENCE

There are over 350 solitaire games that can be played with cards. The most common is called Canfield, or Klondike. Others include Ali Baba, Aztec Pyramids, Four-Leaf Clovers, House on the Hill, Shah of Persia, Spider, Thermometer, and Royal Families. There are also solitaire games meant to be played by two people, which is odd since *solitaire* means "alone."

CASSE-TÊTE CHINOIS
de Cinq Cents Figures Symétriques

A CHINESE PUZZLE-BRAIN
Consisting of a Five hundred symmetrical figures.

QUEBRADERO DE CABEZA
Juego Chino de Quinientos figuras simétricas.

增補七巧戲

# HIPPOPOTAMUS

## Equipment

- 1 sheet of kraft paper (at least 10 x 14 inches)
- 1 piece of green fabric (at least 10 x 14 inches)
- 1 sheet of tagboard (1/8 inch thick)
- plastic folder or soup spoon
- dice
- popsicle sticks
- kitchen string
- white poster paint
- brush
- felt-tip pens or fabric paints
- pencil
- fabric glue
- strong glue
- pinking shears
- scissors
- X-acto knife

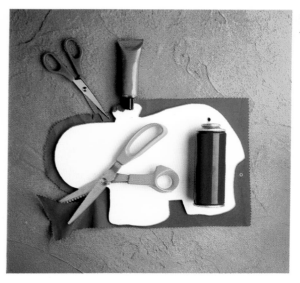

**2**

**1**

Draw the shape of a large round animal (a hippopotamus, for example) on the kraft paper and cut it out. Trace this shape onto the tagboard and cut it out carefully with the knife. Be sure to protect the table underneath with a piece of cardboard or wood.

## TO GLUE:

**Apply glue to the entire surface. Spread the tagboard with fabric glue, smoothing it with a piece of cardboard.**

Spray glue on the animal shape and place it on the fabric. Smooth the surface with the folder. Use pinking shears to cut around the shape, leaving about 1/2 inch of extra fabric. Notch every inch with the regular scissors, so that the fabric will fold under smoothly. Place a line of glue on the edge of the fabric and on the tagboard. Glue the edges of the fabric all around the tagboard.

**3**

With the felt-tip pen, outline the animal and any designs that will appear on it. Color the inside of the designs with felt-tip pens.

**4**

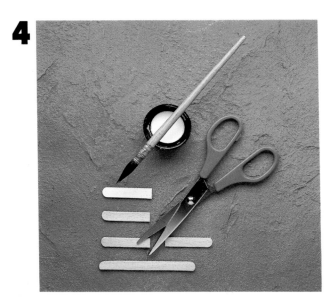

Cut 25 popsicle sticks in half and paint both sides white.

**5**

Glue the sticks vertically to the edge of the animal shape. Space them evenly. Measure the circumference of the animal; double the circumference and add 8 inches to determine the length of string needed. After cutting string, fold it in half and loop it around one of the sticks. Twist the string 3 or 4 times, wind it around the next stick, and continue around the edge until all the sticks have been wound. When the end is reached, make a strong knot around the first stick. Cut the ends of the string and glue them down.

## GENERAL RULES

The player who throws the highest number on the dice starts the game. Play proceeds clockwise from one player to the next. Any dice that fall on the floor or land on an edge must be thrown again. See rules for two dice games on page 30; consult a book of dice games for others.

# FABRIC AND FOAM

## Equipment

- 3–4 feet of foam pipe insulation (1 1/2 inches in diameter)
- 1 piece of cotton fabric (3 feet x 6 inches)
- 1 piece of self-adhesive felt (or regular felt and fabric glue)
- shoe box cover
- glue
- scissors

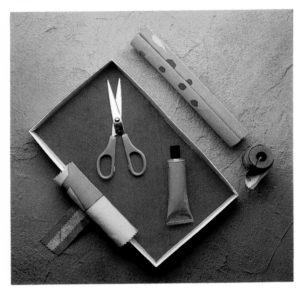

**Foam insulation for pipes is available at plumbing supply stores and large hardware stores. Other soft tubing can also be used.**

Cut a length of foam pipe insulation equal to the circumference (the distance around the outside edge) of the box cover. Slip one finger through the cut side to open the insulation. Place it, with the slot in the middle, on top of the fabric. Push the edges of the fabric inside the slot. Use the scissors to help. Leave about 1/2 inch of material on each end of the insulation. Fold these carefully into the inside, then set aside fabric-covered insulation. Cut a rectangle of felt to the dimensions of the box. Remove the protective backing and attach it to the inside bottom of the box. Place glue on the inside

and outside edges of the sides of the box and place the sleeve on it. Pull open the sleeve slightly, so that the glue is between the 2 thicknesses of foam. To finish, glue a 2-inch strip of fabric or felt to the joint as shown in the photograph.

# TREE

## Equipment
- 1 pound air-drying plastic clay
- red and green self-adhesive felt (or regular felt and fabric glue)
- glossy green and brown poster paints
- brush
- hole punch and hammer
- knife
- rolling pin

straighten it up so that it forms a rim around the edge of the leaves.

Let dry at least 24 hours. When completely dry, paint.

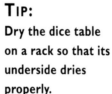

**TIP:**
**Dry the dice table on a rack so that its underside dries properly.**

Knead the clay to make it soft. Roll three-quarters of the dough to about 1/8 inch thick. Cut out the shape of the tree with a knife. The leaves should fit inside a 7-inch square and the trunk should be about 7 inches long. Trim excess and cut a second, thicker piece of dough the same size as the trunk. Place this over the trunk and use the back of the knife to draw lines for the bark. Cut a long strip (1 1/4 inches wide) of clay and attach it on its edge around the tree top, pinching it to attach it to the base. Smooth the strip around the bottom and

Place the tree on the felt and draw the shape of the leaves. Cut it out carefully with scissors. (It will have to be cut a little smaller than the outline to fit inside the leaf area.) Punch holes in the felt, then glue it to the bottom of the dice table. Cut out circles in the red felt and glue them in the holes in the green felt.

**T**he Greek philosopher Plato attributed the invention of dice to the Egyptian god Thoth, god of wisdom and learning. There are numerous games to play with dice. Here are two:

## ROUND THE CLOCK

Using a pair of dice, players try to roll the numbers from 1 to 12, in sequence. The value of one die or the total of the two may be counted. A player who needs a 3 can throw either a 1 and a 2 or a 3 and any other number. The first player to reach 12 wins.

## PIG

*Pig* is played with one die. Before the game starts each player throws the die. The player who rolls the lowest number takes the first turn. Each player in turn throws the die and records the number shown. The same player can throw the die as many times as he or she wants, continuing to add the numbers rolled, but if the player rolls a one, all the points scored for that turn are lost. Each player throws the die until he or she decides to stop or rolls a one. The first player to score a total of 101 wins.

## THE ROYAL GAME OF UR

The royal game of Ur, named after the city in which it was discovered, is one of the oldest known games. More than four thousand years old, it was found by archaeologists in Iraq (formerly Mesopotamia) in 1920. Its game board is beautifully inlaid with twenty squares of lapis lazuli and mother-of-pearl. Each player had seven pieces, whose movements were determined by throws of six pyramid-shaped dice. The inlaid design showed a number of different designs. Each player tried to cover all the squares of one design with his or her own pieces while preventing an opponent from doing the same thing.

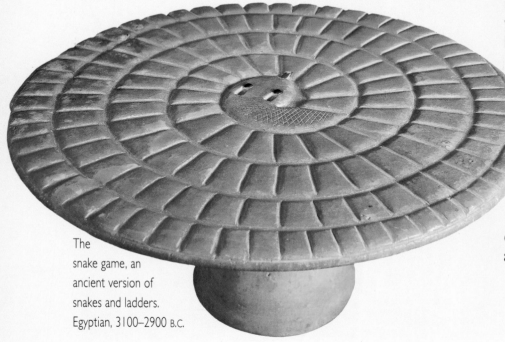

The snake game, an ancient version of snakes and ladders. Egyptian, 3100–2900 B.C.

# DICE: THE OLDEST GAME EQUIPMENT IN THE WORLD

No one knows how long ago people began to play with dice. They are so old that thousands of years ago their origins were already unknown.
Dice appear in ancient mythologies and in the Bible.
Before six-sided dice were invented, people threw two-sided sticks. Cowrie shells were used as dice in some parts of the world. So were knucklebones, which are small bones from the feet of dogs and sheep.
The Romans used dice that looked like modern ones—cubes with six sides—but they also used knucklebones. Other early dice, including the ones used to play senet (see below), were pyramid shaped, and could have four or more sides.
Dice have been discovered in tombs and burial sites all over the world. So have loaded dice—dice meant for cheating.

Three dice from the necropolis (burial ground) of Osteria, Rome. Sixth century B.C.

# DOMINOES

*Dominoes*, introduced into Europe by Marco Polo in the sixteenth century, was a favorite game in monasteries. The monks preferred it to dice, a game often associated with bandits and thieves. The name is said to have originated from the expression *domino gratias* (grace rendered to God).

# EGYPTIAN SENET

This game was popular for over one thousand years. Archaeologists have discovered numerous senet boards in ancient Egyptian tombs. In Tutankhamen's tomb, a wall painting shows the pharaoh playing senet.
Senet was played on a board of thirty squares, called houses, arranged in a pattern of three rows with ten houses in each. The game symbolized the journey to the underworld, the land of the dead. Senet was played with two-sided sticks used like dice. Players moved their game pieces from square 1, "death," to square 26, "the place of mummification." Once all of a player's pieces arrived on this square, the pieces could continue to move to the last square, which symbolized everlasting life. So, senet had religious significance, but is also recognizable as a kind of early backgammon.

# SNAKES AND LADDERS

*The old game of snakes and ladders is still known by that name in England. In the United States, however, manufacturers discovered that many people didn't want to buy a game with the word* snakes *in the title. So, the game acquired a new name and a slightly different look. We know it as* chutes and ladders *or* slides and ladders, *and it is one of the classic childhood board games.*

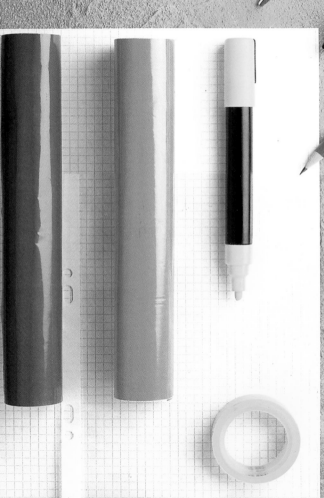

# PAGE DIVIDER
# CHECKERBOARD

## Equipment

- 1 clear plastic protector for notebook
- 1 piece of steel window screen
- 1 sheet of graph paper (that fits into protector)
- heavy plastic colored tape
- 1 magnetized metal plate (or self-sticking magnetic squares or magnetic tape)
- 2 small pieces of colored contact paper (or construction paper if self-sticking magnets are used)
- permanent felt-tip pen (to write on plastic)
- pencil
- scissors
- punch and hammer (if using magnetic plate)
- ruler

**IMPORTANT:**
The photographs in this section show French checkerboards, which have one hundred squares; an American checkerboard has sixty-four. Also, the U.S. board has a dark square in the lower left-hand corner and a light square in the lower right-hand corner.

Fold the graph paper in half vertically and horizontally to find the middle. From the center, count 4 squares on either side of the center. Beginning with the lower left-hand corner, color in every other square, alternating on the following line. When there are 8 lines, the grid is ready.

Slide the paper into the plastic protector and paint over the squares with the felt-tip pen. Remove the sheet of paper from the plastic protector and slip the screen in.

Measure the dimensions of the plastic protector (not including the edge with holes). Cut a rectangle of the same size from the screening. Put colored tape around the edges of the screen.

**2**

Attach 2 strips of colored contact paper to the metal sheet, 1 color to each half. Use the hammer and punch to cut out 12 pieces from each color. If using magnetic squares or tape, attach colored paper to adhesive and cut out 12 pieces from each color. Remember to put a piece of wood under the punch to protect the work surface.

The magnetized pieces will stick to the window screening.

T he window screening must be made of steel; the magnetic pieces won't stick to aluminum screen. Take a magnet to the store when buying the screen and be sure that the magnet sticks.

# MATCHBOX CHECKERBOARD

### Equipment

- 1 sheet tagboard (1/8 inch thick)
- 1 sheet of anti-reflecting Plexiglas, cut to the dimensions of the finished checkerboard (available in framing stores or in the framing section of department stores)
- 64 small matchboxes
- 12–16 walnuts
- 1 1/2 pounds green lentils or dried peas
- 1 1/2 pounds of small white beans
- red and green poster paint
- spray paint
- brush
- cloth tape (1/2 inch wide)
- glue
- X-acto knife
- knife
- ruler

might require an extra pair of hands, so ask some-one for help. Press the tape firmly all around.

If matchboxes are not available, use another kind of small box. The boxes must all be the same size, and the piece of tagboard must be large enough to hold them.

Open and empty all the matchboxes. Only the bottom section will be used. With the X-acto knife, cut the tagboard to the correct size. To determine the correct size, measure 1 matchbox. The tagbord must be 8 times the width and 8 times the length of a matchbox. Put glue on the bottom and sides of all the boxes and attach them to the tagboard; there will be 8 rows of 8 match-boxes. Spray-paint the boxes. Let dry and spray another coat.

Carefully use the knife to split the walnuts and take out the nuts. Ask an adult for help with this. Paint 12 shells red and 12 shells green. Let them dry.

Fill alternate boxes with lentils and white beans. (Remember that the lower left-hand corner of a checker board is always the darker square.) Place the Plexiglas on the surface of the checkerboard and attach it with tape all around the sides. This

**TIP:**
**The plastic may develop static electricity because of the dry beans. To prevent this, put a few drops of salad oil on a paper towel and rub the underside of the plastic before attaching it to the checkerboard.**

**W**hen spray-painting, don't forget to cover the working surface. Work in a well-ventilated area—a garage or basement, if possible.

# CHECKERS ON A BEACH MAT

**Equipment**
- 1 straw mat (sometimes called a *tatami*)
- sponge cloth or thin artificial sponges (2 colors)
- acrylic paint
- brush
- felt-tip pen
- scissors
- ruler

Draw a 16-inch square on the mat. Then draw a grid with 8 squares on each side, each 2 inches wide. Paint alternate squares of the grid, starting with the first square on the bottom left.
Draw and cut out 12 circles from each piece of sponge cloth (24 in all). Trace the inside of a roll of tape to make the circles or trace around a large coin.

# CHECKERS IN THE SAND

**Equipment**
- 64 small stones
- 24 flat shells

Gather 32 light stones and 32 dark stones. They should all be about the same size. Then find 24 shells—12 light and 12 dark—to use as checker pieces.
Arrange the stones on the sand in a checkerboard pattern and use the shells as pieces.

**TIP:**
If it's a windy day, dip the checker pieces in water to keep them from blowing away. Let them dry before storing them.

## CHECKERS

Checkers—called *draughts* in England—probably originated in the Far East, but games resembling checkers have been played in many countries for thousands of years. Checkerboards and pieces have been discovered in the tombs of the Egyptian pharaohs (from about 1600 B.C.), and an Egyptian vase shows a lion and an antelope playing a version of checkers.

It's hard to know when checkers was first played because the earliest games might have been played with stones, shells, or bones as pieces, but by the early eighteenth century, the game had taken its modern form . At the same time it was developing numerous variations in different places. Many versions of checkers now exist.

*International checkers* (also called *Polish checkers*), uses a board of one hundred squares. Each player has twenty pieces, not twelve, and some of the rules of the game are different from American checkers—for instance, pieces can jump forward and backward, even before they become kings.

For *Turkish checkers*, each player begins with two rows of eight pieces, placed on the second and third rows. The pieces move horizontally and vertically instead of diagonally, on both black and white squares.

Other variations include *diagonal checkers*, played from corner to corner on a standard checkerboard, and *losing checkers*, the goal of which is to be the first player to have no pieces left on the board.

Most of the variants of checkers are played with a standard checkerboard and checkers, so anyone who enjoys the game can look up the rules and play the different versions.

Bone chess piece from the twelfth century.

## CHESS

Chess, a game of mock warfare in which two armies attempt to win by capturing each other's king, may have originated in India. A variation of the game existed there under the name of *chaturanga*, which means "the game of four kings." It was played on a square chessboard with sixty-four squares. The pieces included a ship, a horse, a king, and four pawns. *Chaturanga* was a game for four people. The players threw dice to determine which piece to move, so it was a game of chance as well as a game of strategy. Modern chess is a game of pure strategy.

The word *chess* comes from *shah*, the Persian word for "king." *Checkmate* comes from *shah mat*, which means "the king is dead." The game of chess that we play today is a descendant of the Persian game *shatranj*, brought from India by Persian traders.

The rules of chess assumed their modern form around 1500.

Box lid showing a game of chess.

## THE FAKE CHESS MACHINE

In 1770, a German, the Baron von Kempelen, became famous throughout Europe for his invention of a machine called "the Turk," which could beat all the great chess masters. The baron and his machine enjoyed great success until the day his trick was unmasked. A man was hidden inside! A real chess machine was not invented until 1958, when the first computer chess program was developed.

## THE MEANING OF GAMES

Games can tell us about the beliefs, values, or worries of the people who play them.

Senet (page 31) is an example of this. So is *mancala*, played in Africa and India. Perhaps the oldest known game, mancala is a game of planting and reaping. The player who finishes with the most "food" wins.

In the middle of the nineteenth century, a board game called The Mansion of Happiness was produced in the United States. The game rewarded players for landing on spaces marked with virtues such as honesty and generosity, and punished players for landing on cruelty and cheating. The winner was the first player to arrive at the middle of the board, the Mansion of Happiness. At that time many Americans believed games were a waste of time, but parents could be convinced to buy a game that taught children to behave well.

In the 1930s, when the Great Depression caused numerous people to become poor, many new money games were developed. That was the decade Monopoly became a bestseller.

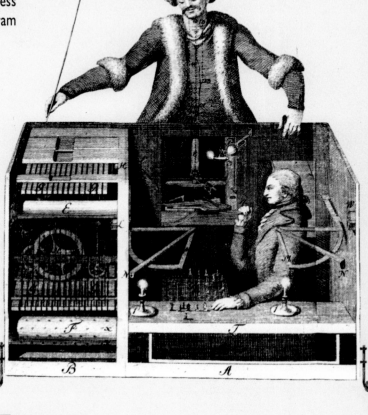

*The Chess Players*, by Eugene Delacroix, 1847.

*In North Africa, a unique variation of checkers developed, called dâmna, which is played primarily by the people of the Sahara. Dâmna consists of a checkerboard with nine squares on each side. Forty tall pieces (called male pieces) and forty round stones, nuts, or dates (called female pieces) are placed on it. The pieces can be moved as the players wish, but may not be moved backwards or remain on the same line.*

# CLAY BATTLE

## Equipment
- 2 square clay tiles (8 inches)
- a wooden crate or 6-foot furring strip (Furring strips are available at lumber yards.)
- 1 pound air-drying plastic clay
- 8 corks, trimmed to square corners
- small finishing nails
- 1 sheet of sandpaper
- 1 sheet of plain paper
- wooden toothpicks
- red and blue thin colored tape
- red and blue cloth tape
- red and blue poster paint
- paint brushes
- pencil
- permanent felt-tip pen
- wood glue
- X-acto knife
- small saw
- apple corer
- rolling pin and board
- ruler

**1**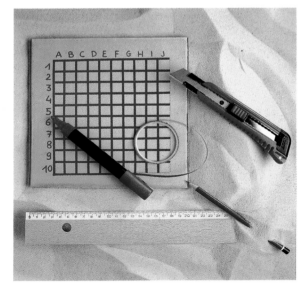

Trace a 6 1/4-inch square in the center of 1 square tile. Draw a grid with a hundred 5/8-inch squares, 10 on each side. Place a strip of thin red tape on each line and a strip all around the outside edge. Use the felt-tip pen to mark the numbers and letters (see photograph). Make a second grid on the other tile, this time using blue tape.

**2**

To make the pieces, roll the clay to about 1/8 inch thick with the rolling pin. (If the clay is too hard, moisten it and knead it before rolling.) Use the apple corer to make small rounds of clay. Put them on a piece of wood or cardboard to dry. Repeat several times until there are at least 100 pieces.

**3**

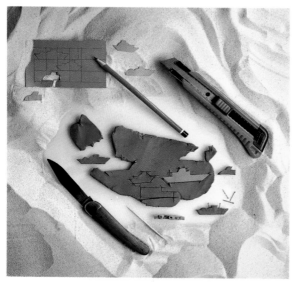

To make the boats: draw a grid on a piece of paper, making 5/8-inch squares. Draw a submarine that fits into 1 square; then draw a cruiser that fits into 2 squares, a destroyer that fits into 3 squares, and an aircraft carrier that fits into 4 squares. Cut out a rectangle for the deck of the aircraft carrier (1/2 x 2 squares). Cut out each paper pattern and place them on the rolled-out clay. Use the knife to cut out the shapes of the ships. Make two complete fleets of ten ships each.

**Each player has a fleet of 10 ships:**
**1 aircraft carrier,**
**2 destroyers,**
**3 cruisers,**
**4 submarines.**

Insert finishing nails for the guns. Moisten the aircraft deck and attach it to the aircraft carrier. With a toothpick, make holes in each ship. Make one hole for each of the squares they cover—a submarine should have 1 hole; the cruiser, 2; and so on. The holes must be positioned so that each is on a different square when the game is set up for play (see photograph).

Let the ships dry flat, but put the aircraft on its base so the deck does not bend.

**4**

The boats and pieces will be dry after 48 hours. To keep them from breaking, paint them when dry with a mixture made of 2 tablespoons of water and 1 tablespoon of wood glue.

To make the flags, cut toothpicks into 1-inch lengths. Cut small strips of cloth tape and wrap one around each toothpick, then cut the tape to make a triangular flag. Make 20 red and 20 blue flags.

Make sure the ships are stable; if not, rub the bottoms with a piece of fine sandpaper. Paint 1 set of ships and 40 round pieces red; paint the other set of ships blue. The rest of the round pieces are left unpainted. They are "neutral" pieces.

**PLAYING HINT:**

When an opponent's ship has been sunk, place neutral pieces in the squares that surround the sunken ship. Because the ships may not touch, these spaces cannot contain a ship.

# RULES OF THE GAME

Each player has a grid with 10 squares on a side, numbered 1 to 10 vertically and A to J horizontally. Each player also has a fleet of 10 ships, which are described on page 42, and positions his or her ships on the grid. The ships must not touch each other. Each player then attacks in turn, by specifying a square on the opponent's grid. The player places a neutral piece on the square if no ship has been hit, or a red piece if the opponent says "hit." A ship is "sunk" when all the squares it occupies have been hit.

When one's own ship is hit, place a flag of the opponent's color on the ship. When one hits an opponent's ship that is on the same square as one of one's own ships, place a flag of one's own color. The player who first sinks the opponent's fleet wins the game.

Players must not be able to see the location of each other's ships during the game. To construct the wooden frame shown in the photographs, cut the furring strip into eight 8 1/4-inch lengths. Sand rough parts. Glue strips together at the corners with wood glue, glue a cork into each corner, let dry, and paint the frames. When dry, insert tile in each.

# Notebook Battle

## Equipment
- 2 notebook dividers
- 2 sheets of contact paper (erasable)
- 1 black indelible pen
- 4 erasable felt-tip pens (different colors)
- 2 colors of plastic tape (optional)

Cut a piece of contact paper to the size of the divider and attach the paper to the divider. With the black pen, draw a grid with 100 squares (10 on each side). Place 2 strips of plastic tape along the side and top of the grid, and mark them with the letters and numbers as shown. Each player has 2 pens—one to mark his or her captures, the other to mark ships captured by the opponent.

# Small Stones

## Equipment
- 80 small stones
- 2 felt-tip pens (different colors)

Using one of the felt-tip pens, mark the numbers 1 through 10 and the letters A through J on 20 of the stones. On 20 other stones, mark one side with an X and the other with a circle. Repeat with the other color and the other 40 stones.
Draw a grid in the sand. Place the lettered and numbered stones to form the top and side of the grid. Arrange the ships—1 aircraft carrier of 4 stones, 2 destroyers of 3 stones each, 3 cruisers of 2 stones each, and 4 submarines of 1 stone each—with the circle side of each stone up.

When a ship has been hit, turn the stone so that the X side is facing up. To mark a hit on an opponent's ship, make a cross in the sand. Players keep track of their attempts that miss by marking a point with a finger in the sand.

**S**trategy is part of the vocabulary of war. The word comes from the Greek word for a military general. Strategy games require skill and the ability to plan ahead.

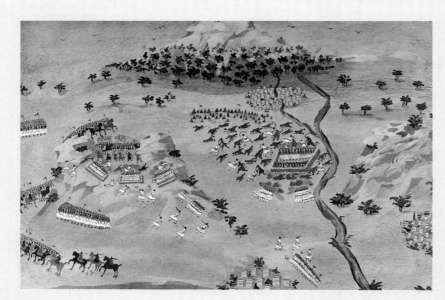

*Go has been played in China since 2000 B.C. It was called wei-qui or wei-chi. In Korea it was known as pa-tuk. In A.D. 735, Emperor Kibidaijin brought go to Japan, where it was so successful that it became a favorite game among the aristocracy and was taught in military academies.*

## THE GAME OF GO

Go is Japan's most popular game, but it is also the game played most seriously by adults—as chess is the United States and Europe. An expert go player is called a "master" and can earn a good income playing the game at competitions.

The rules of go are simple, although the strategy is not. The board has nineteen vertical and nineteen horizontal lines, which form 361 intersections. The game is played on these intersections with 181 black and 180 white flat, round pieces. Placing one piece on the board at a time, the two players must surround the maximum amount of territory. The winner is the player who controls more of the board at the end of the game.

The strategy of go is similar to military strategy. Two opposing sides attempt to control territory and surround each other's troops. In Japanese, go means both "game of encircling" and "control of the territory."

Illustration of a game of go in Japan.

## MONOPOLY

Monopoly was developed and copyrighted in 1933 by Charles Darrow, who was unemployed at the time. Marketed in the middle of the Depression, this board game became an amazing success. Making a game out of high-level financial dealings gave people the chance to escape their fears about their real financial situation. Needless to say, Monopoly rescued Darrow from his poverty by becoming the most famous and widely sold game in the world. What many people don't know, however, is that Monopoly was based on The Landlord's Game, created by Elizabeth J. Magie in 1904. Darrow had played a modified version of the game with friends. He didn't invent Monopoly; he just perfected a game that already existed.

## ROLE-PLAYING GAMES

In 1973, Gary Gigax, a shoemaker in Wisconsin, invented the first role-playing game, based on the medieval and fantastic world created by J. R. R. Tolkien in *Lord of the Rings*. The game, Dungeons and Dragons, was enormously successful. Sword and sorcery role-playing games were especially popular in the 1980s and have now influenced board games and video games.

A scene from *The Go Master*, a play by the famous Japanese writer Yasunari Kawabata.

## A DATING GAME

In the United States, many people believe that games are just for children—chess is one of the few exceptions. Other cultures take their games more seriously.

In the country of Madagascar, for instance, a man who wishes to marry might be challenged to a game of *fanoroma* by his future father-in-law. The young man is not required to win the game, but he must play well, showing that he understands strategy and the importance of planning ahead. Someone who plays carelessly would not be considered a good choice as a husband.

The game of go was brought to Europe in the 1920s, and it became especially popular after the Second World War. The game is now played throughout the world, but Japan—with ten million players—remains the capital of go.

# BICYCLE WHEEL

## Equipment
- bicycle
- 1 piece of cardboard or plastic
- small paper balls, pebbles, or small candies (one color per player)
- 1 large metal or plastic drawing clip
- indelible-ink pen
- 5 rolls plastic or cloth tape (different colors)
- scissors

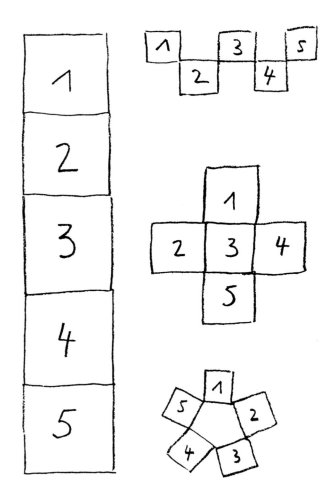

Decorate the rim of a bicycle wheel with strips of colored tape (one space corresponds to the distance between 2 spokes). On the tape, write the numbers 1 through 5 two times. Cut an arrow from the cardboard and decorate it. Attach it with the clip to one bar of the front fork of the bicycle.

## RULES OF THE GAME

Draw 5 squares on the ground (in any pattern) and number them 1 to 5. Players put their bets on one or more squares. A player spins the wheel. The player who bets on the square corresponding to the number that comes up on the bicycle wheel is the winner. If 2 players bet on the same square, they share the winnings. If there is no winner, all the players share the winnings.

# Tick-tack-toe

### Equipment
- round cheese box
- white and colored contact paper
- 1 piece of paper
- suction dart
- old felt-tip pen (dried out)
- caps from 3 felt-tip pens
- bead
- florist's wire
- yellow and black permanent-ink felt-tip pens
- cloth tape
- glue
- scissors
- X-acto knife
- hammer and punch or awl
- ruler

Punch out a hole in the middle of the cheese box bottom. Make a corresponding hole in the top of the box. Close the box and attach tape around the side.

Cover the top with white contact paper and divide it into 12 equal sections. Decorate each section with colored contact paper, as shown. In the white sections, draw alternating Xs and Os. Color them with the felt-tip pen. Remove the cap, end, and insides from the old felt-tip pen and insert the dart in the pen tube. Cut 2 rings from the felt-tip pen caps. Slip one ring on the felt pen. Bend a piece of wire in half around a pencil to make a loop. Use the pencil to twist the 2 lengths of wire together. Place the wire loop on the felt-tip pen and slip on the second ring. Then slide on the round box. Make two 90° bends in the wire as photograph shows. The wire should extend about 1/2 inch beyond the side of the box and about 1 inch above it. Glue a bead to the end of the wire.

Moisten the tip of the dart and attach it to a table. Spin the wheel to determine which player gets to take the first turn.

# Rules of the Game

This is a game for 2 players, X and O. Players take turns spinning the wheel, but only the player indicated by the ball can put his or her mark on the paper. The object of the game is to make lines of 4 Xs or 4 Os and to prevent one's opponent from completing lines. The lines can be vertical, horizontal, or diagonal. When one player has 4 in a row and draws a line through them, that is worth 1 point. The players agree in advance to play to a particular number of points.

# LUCKY SPIN

### Equipment
- small paper plate
- marble
- small stickers (1/3 inch in diameter, 4 different colors)
- black indelible-ink pen
- 4 felt-tip pens (different colors)
- hammer and punch (or paper hole punch)
- ruler

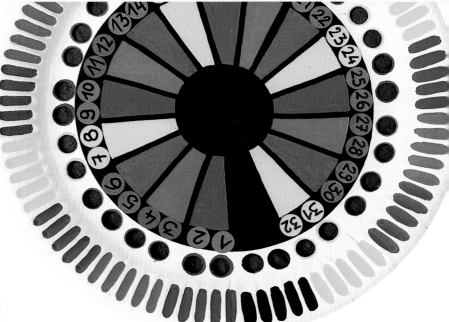

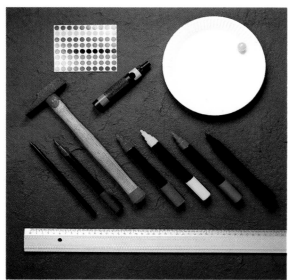

For this game, it's best to use a paper plate with vertical, rather than slanting, grooves around the edge. Color 5 grooves in a row blue, then color 5 red, 5 yellow, and 5 green. Continue this series around the edge. Color any remaining grooves black—this is a neutral area. Using the black felt-tip pen, divide the area in the middle of the plate into sections, as shown, and color them to match the colors on the edge of the plate. Number the stickers (the exact number will depend on the number of grooves on plate). Attach 2 stickers per color division, starting to the right of the black section. Use the punch to make a hole above each sticker. When the plate is spun, the marble will stop in one of the holes.

## RULES OF THE GAME

Any number of players can participate. Players take turns playing the bank. Each player bets on a number. A player spins the plate and the marble stops opposite a number. This is the winning number, and the player who has bet on this number wins; if no player has selected the number, the bank wins. Players can bet with candy, stones, marbles, or cookies.

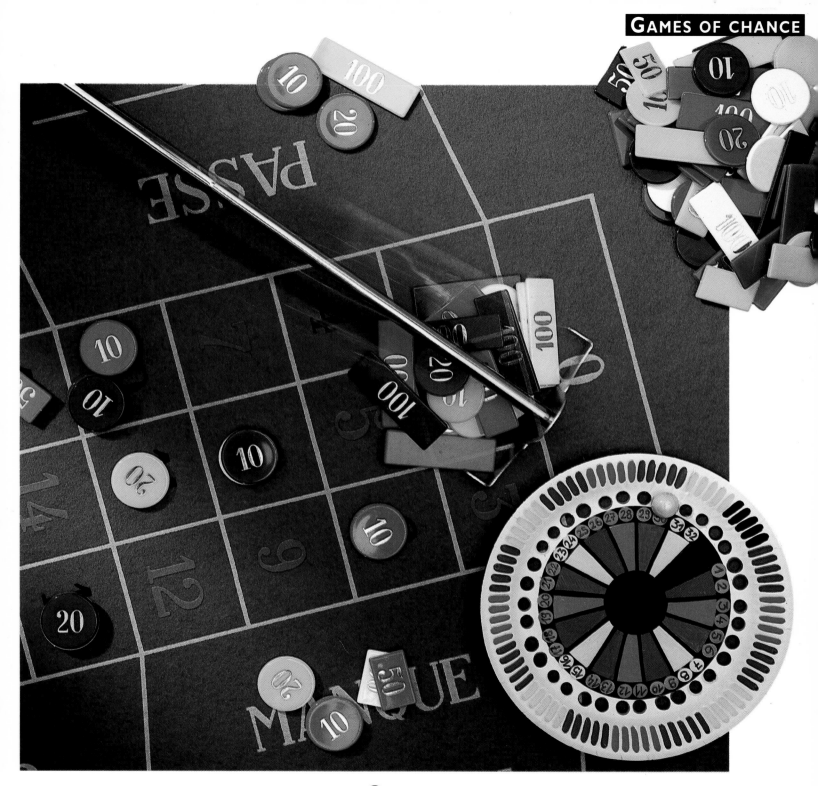

**G**ames of chance have sometimes been considered sacred. Long ago, a tribe of people in the Middle East used to play a dart game. They threw a series of darts, then interpreted the design formed by the darts.

## THE LOTTERY

The lottery is one of the oldest known games of chance. In the Old Testament, God tells Moses to count the people and divide the land by lot. In ancient Rome, Nero entertained his banquet guests by organizing a lottery: the lucky winners were given slaves and houses.

One of the earliest public lotteries was held in Florence, Italy, in 1530, where merchants used it to sell their shops. The principle was simple: the merchant sold tickets, and a lottery was held to determine the new owner, who was then able to set up shop inexpensively.

For hundreds of years governments and other organizations have held lotteries. Early European lotteries raised money for defense and for the poor. In 1878 the U. S. Supreme Court made lotteries illegal because too many people were cheating, but within a hundred years, states were again holding lotteries.

Some people believe public lotteries are good because they allow states to raise money without increasing taxes; other people believe that lotteries encourage gambling and take too much money from the people who can least afford it.

## ACCORDING TO HOYLE

An Englishman named Edmond Hoyle (1672?–1769) is remembered for his books about the rules of games, especially card games, backgammon, and chess. His research was so thorough and so deeply respected that three hundred years after his death, people still say "according to Hoyle" to mean "according to the rules."

Several modern rule books are named after Hoyle. They include games Hoyle never wrote about and many rules that have changed since Hoyle's death.

Chariot race.

## BETTING: AN OLD STORY

Gambling of one kind or another has existed in all historical periods and in all cultures. One common kind of gambling is betting on the outcome of a game or contest between people (such as boxing or football) or animals (such as horse racing).

In Roman times, chariot races were so popular that the *Circus Maximus* was constructed. It was later enlarged so that 250,000 spectators could attend the races. Betting was allowed.

In some places, people bet on the outcomes of fights between animals. Cockfighting (fighting between roosters) is still popular in many countries. Dog fighting, although it's illegal, continues to exist in the United States. In China and Indonesia, there are fights between crickets and flies.

People also bet on animal races—not just on horses and greyhounds, but on camels (in Turkey) and goats (in France), too.

## CASINO BETTING

Casinos (from the Italian *casa*, meaning "house") offer a large number of games of chance.

### Roulette

This is the most popular game in many casinos. Roulette is an ancient game. Although it is a game of chance, players can improve their chances by studying the laws of probability and by using a computer that records the speed of the ball and the wheel. The computer is capable of determining the winning number to within eight figures.

### Slot machines

These machines were invented by an American mechanic, Charles Fey, in 1887. They were first set up in a casino in California, but they quickly became so popular that they can now be found in casinos all over the world.

Slot machines are also called "one-armed bandits." Legend says that the nickname was given by some real bandits who were playing on a machine that was "gaffed"— specially constructed to cheat the players. One of the bandits said, "You sure don't need a gun to hold up anyone, not if you own a couple of machines like these." And the other bandit said, "And this bandit has only one arm." The "arm," of course, is the lever a player pulled to make the older kind of machine work.

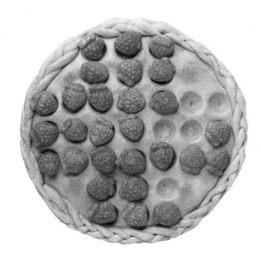

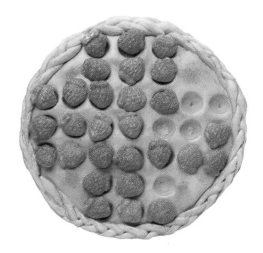

First American edition 1994 published by Ticknor & Fields Books for Young Readers, A Houghton Mifflin company, 215 Park Avenue South, New York, New York 10003. • Copyright © by Hachette, Paris, 1992 • English translation copyright © 1994 by Ticknor & Fields Books for Young Readers • First published in France by Hachette • All rights reserved. • For information about permission to reproduce selections from this book, write to Permissions, Ticknor & Fields, 215 Park Avenue South, New York, New York 10003. • Manufactured in France • The text of this book is set in 13 point Gill Sans

10  9  8  7  6  5  4  3  2  1

Photo credits: © Alinari / Giraudon, page 54 • © Baudry / Explorer • © Edimédia, pages 15, 38, 39 • © Brigitte Enguerand, page 47 • © Giraudon, pages 30, 31, 55 • © Kharbine / Tapabor, page 46 • © Lauros / Giraudon, pages 15, 46 • © Lausat / Explorer, page 38 • © Musée des Arts décoratifs, pages 14, 22, 23 • © Roger-Viollet, page 39 • © de Selva / Tapabor, page 31

---

Library of Congress Cataloging-in-Publication Data

Marchon-Arnaud, Catherine.
    A gallery of games / by Catherine Marchon-Arnaud; photographs by Marc Schwartz; research by Etienne Collomb. — 1st American ed.
       p.    cm. — (Young artisan)
    Includes index.
    Summary: Provides instructions for making beautiful, amusing, or unusual versions of familiar games, including ring toss games, checkers, and roulette wheels.
    ISBN 0-395-68379-3
    1. Handicraft—Juvenile literature.    2. Games—Juvenile literature. [1. Handicraft. 2. Games.] I. Schwartz, Marc, ill.  II. Title.   III. Series.
TT160.M264  1994
745.592—dc20        93-25053      CIP     AC

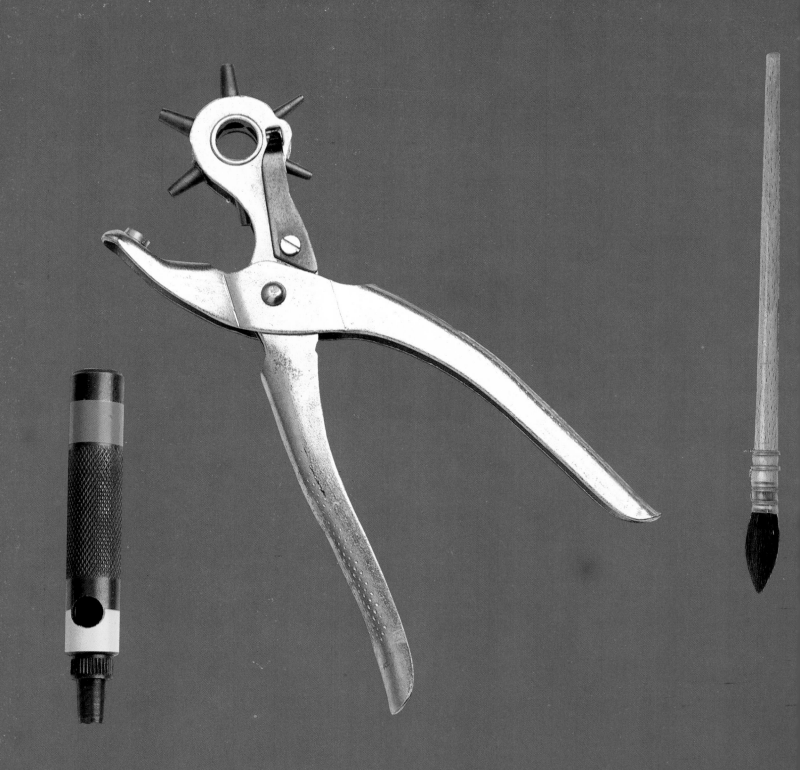